Bell P-39Q
Airacobra

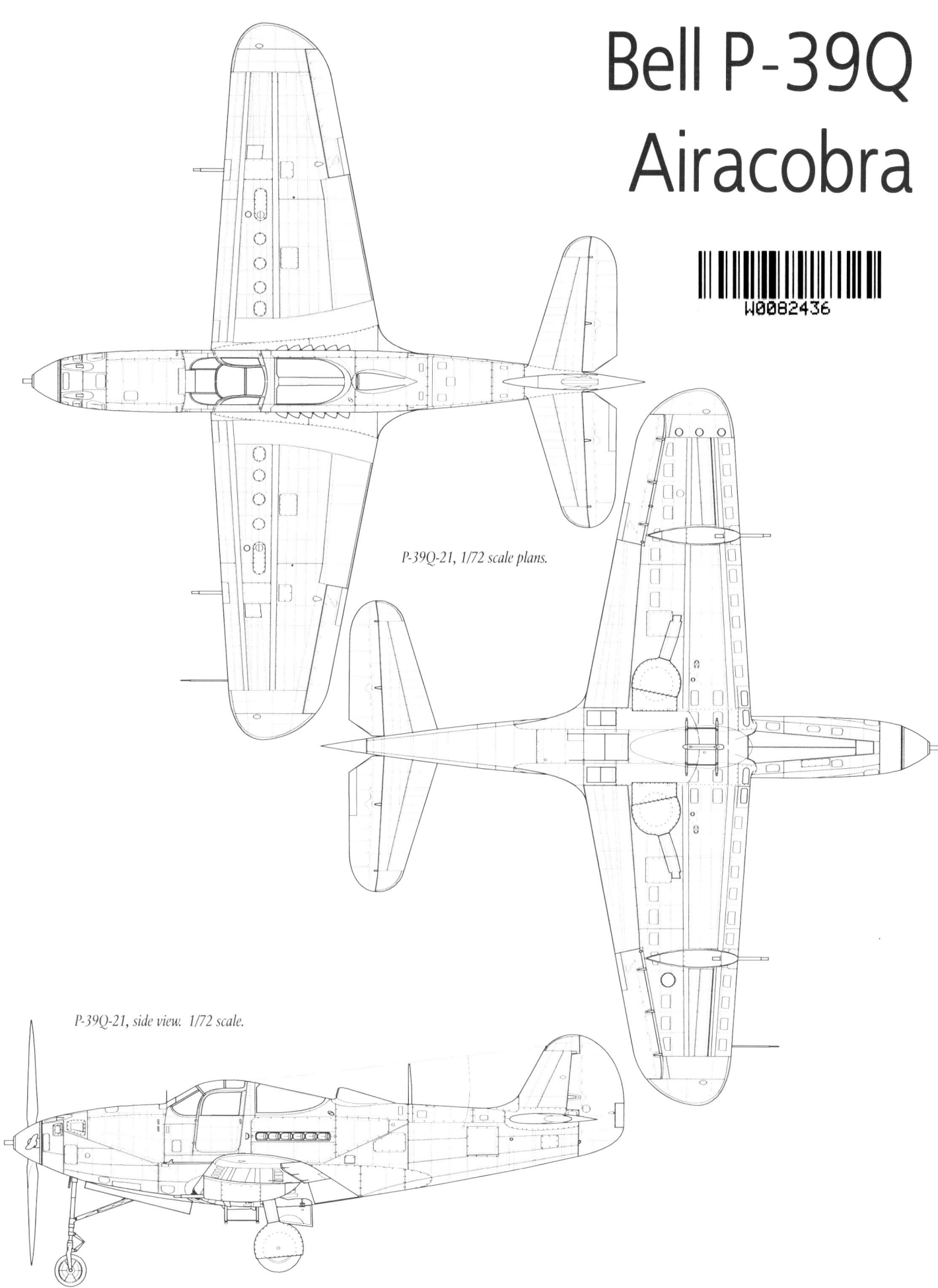

P-39Q-21, 1/72 scale plans.

P-39Q-21, side view. 1/72 scale.

Dariusz Karnas

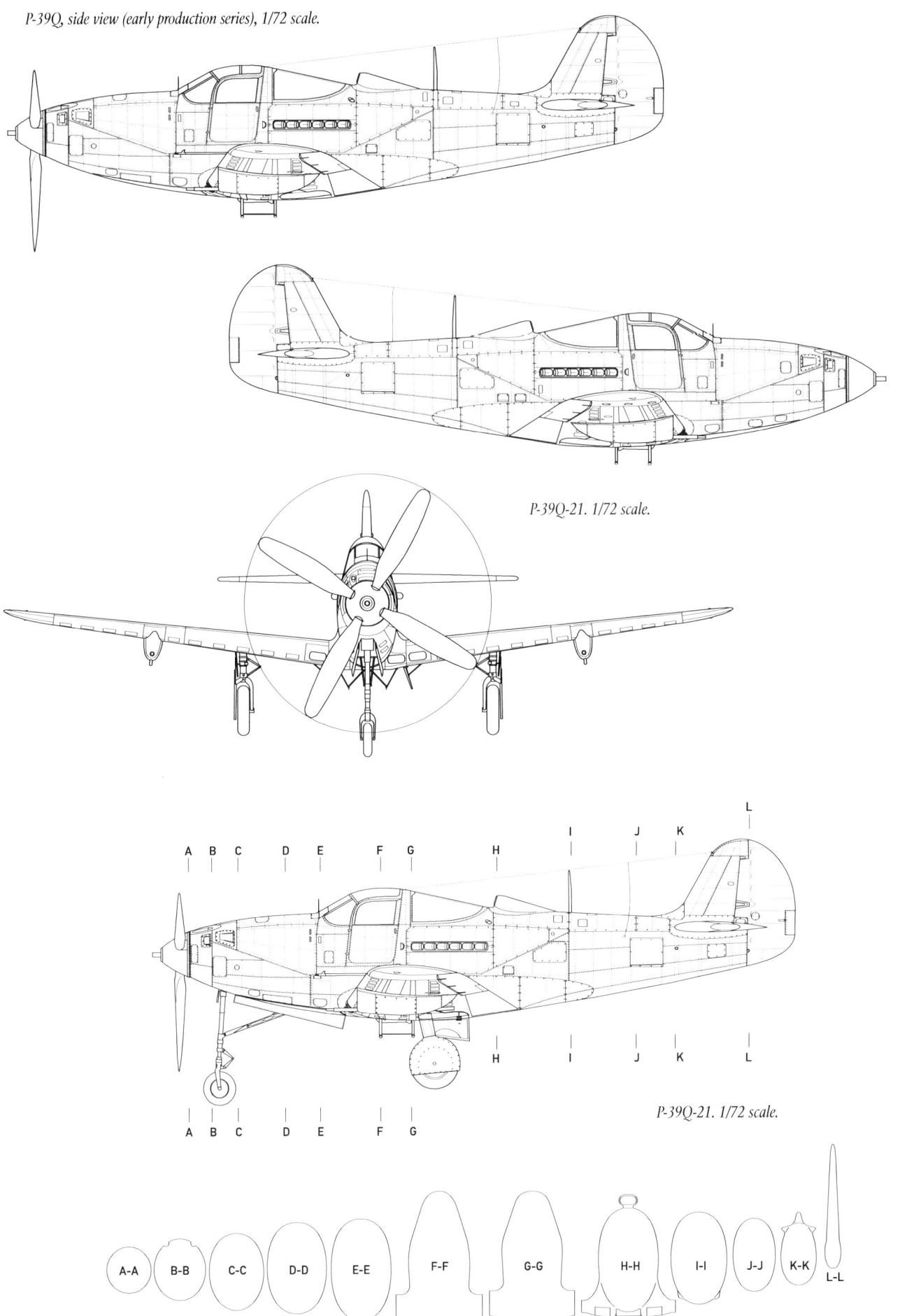

P-39Q, side view (early production series), 1/72 scale.

P-39Q-21. 1/72 scale.

P-39Q-21. 1/72 scale.

A B C D E F G H I J K L

A B C D E F G

H I J K L

A-A B-B C-C D-D E-E F-F G-G H-H I-I J-J K-K L-L

Dariusz Karnas

2

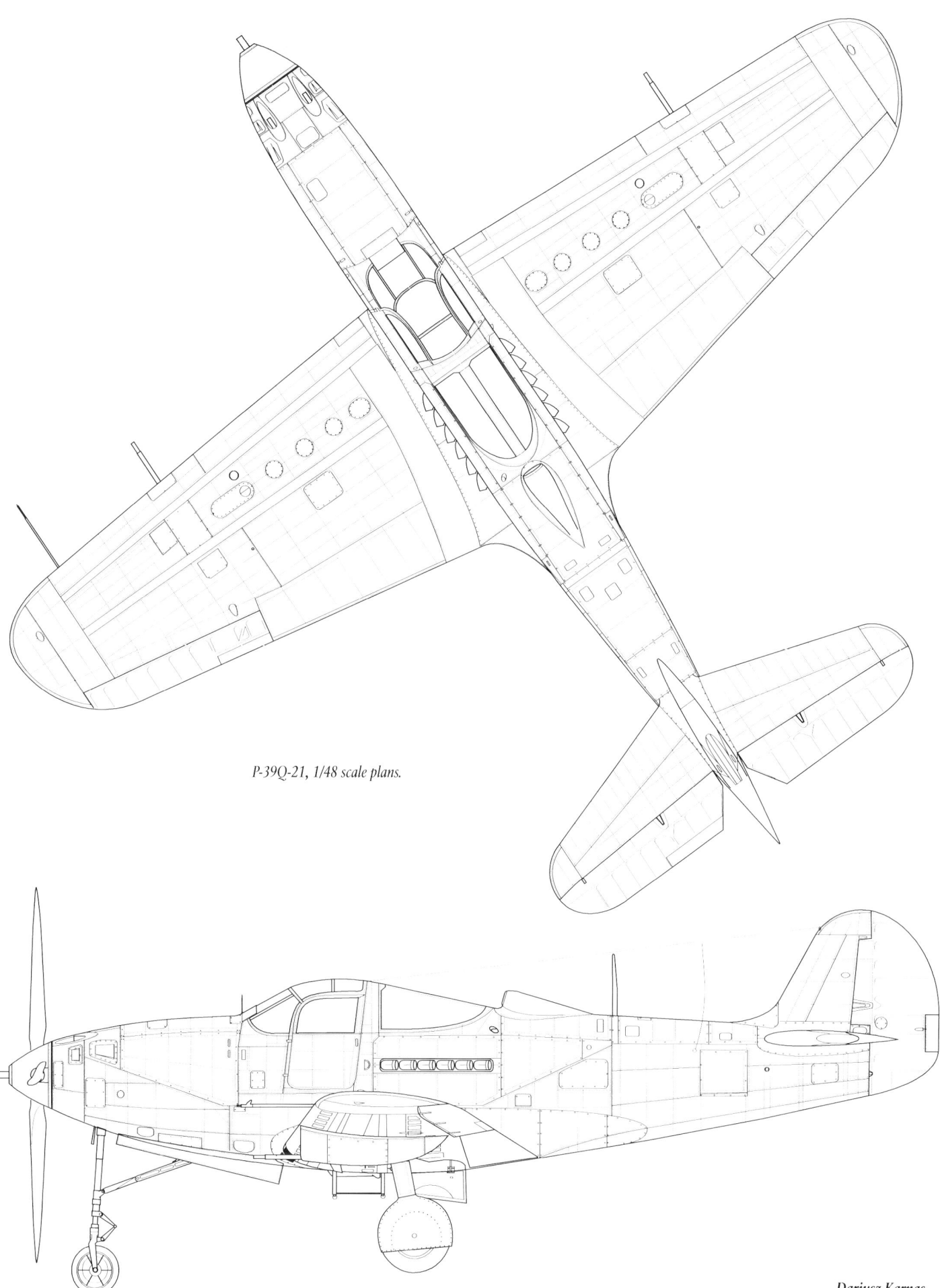

P-39Q-21, 1/48 scale plans.

Dariusz Karnas

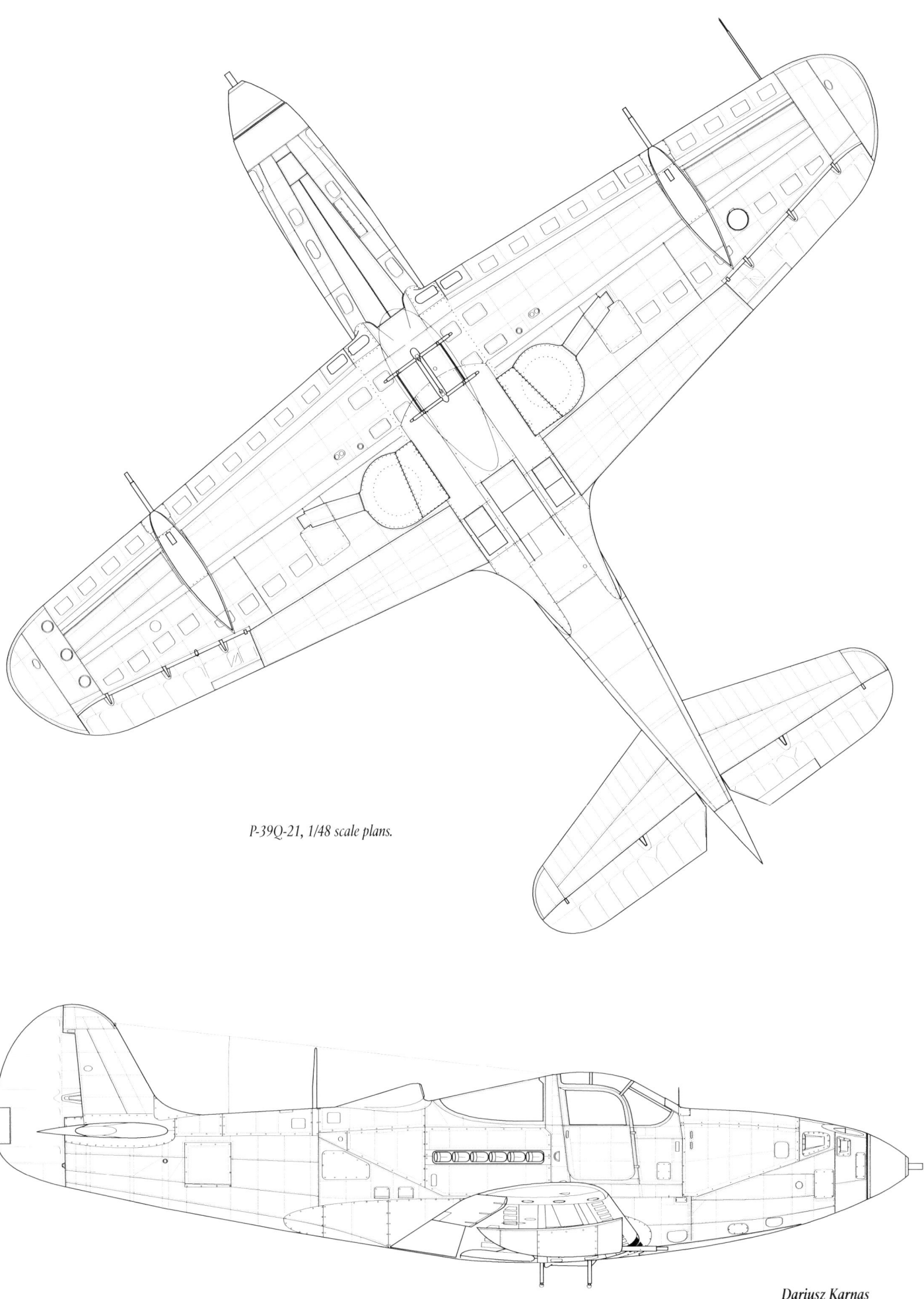

P-39Q-21, 1/48 scale plans.

Dariusz Karnas

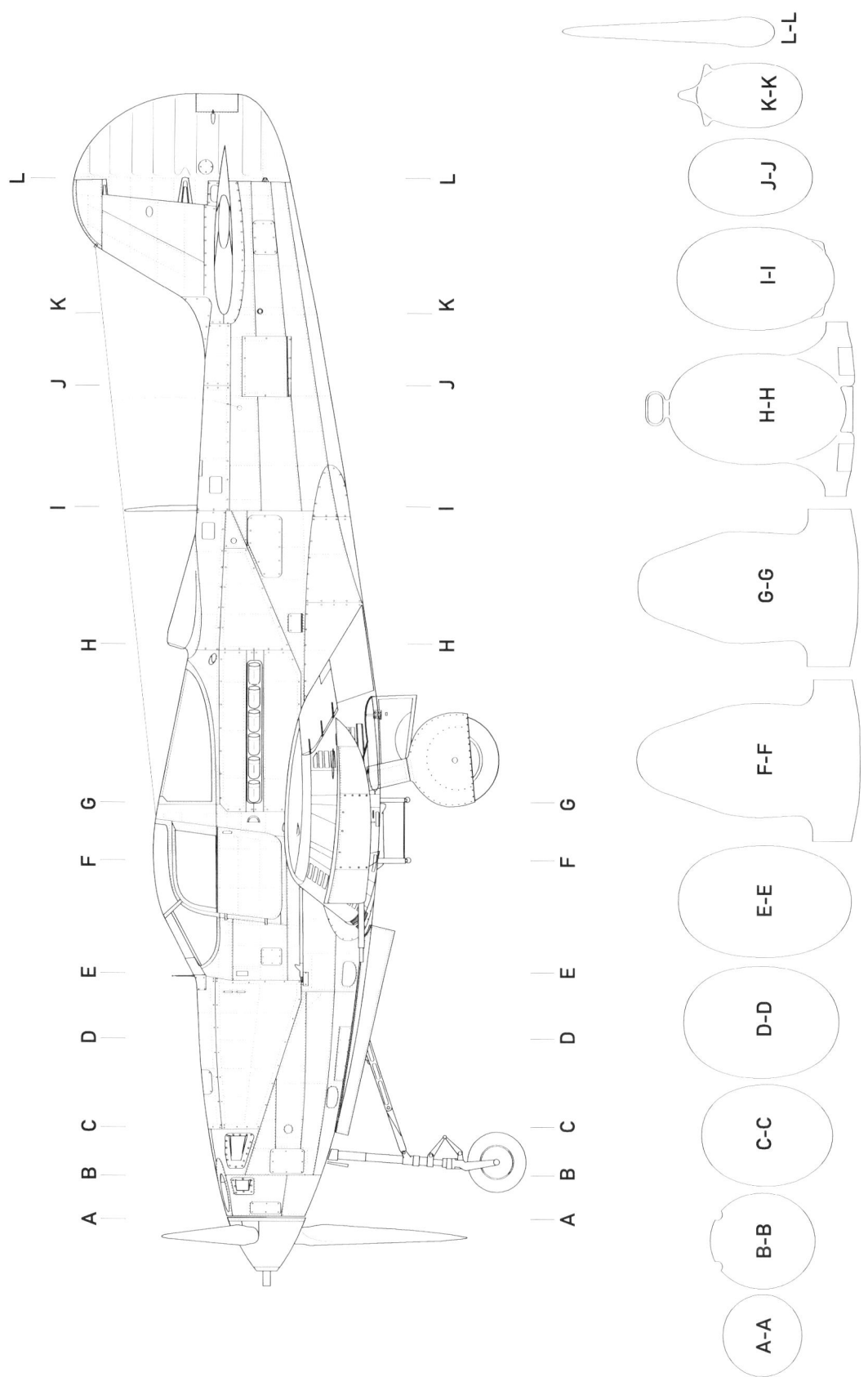

A   B C D E F G H I J K L

A-A B-B C-C D-D E-E F-F G-G H-H I-I J-J K-K L-L

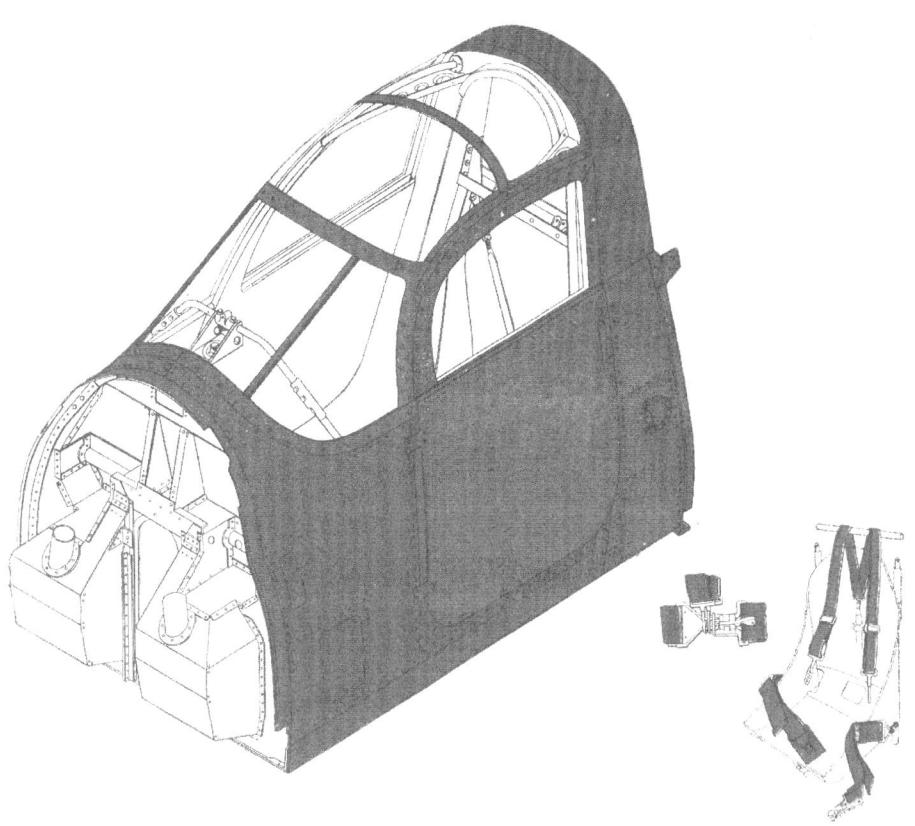

Cockpit arrangement and pilot's seat harness.

Pilot's seat. Drawings from the Technical Manual.

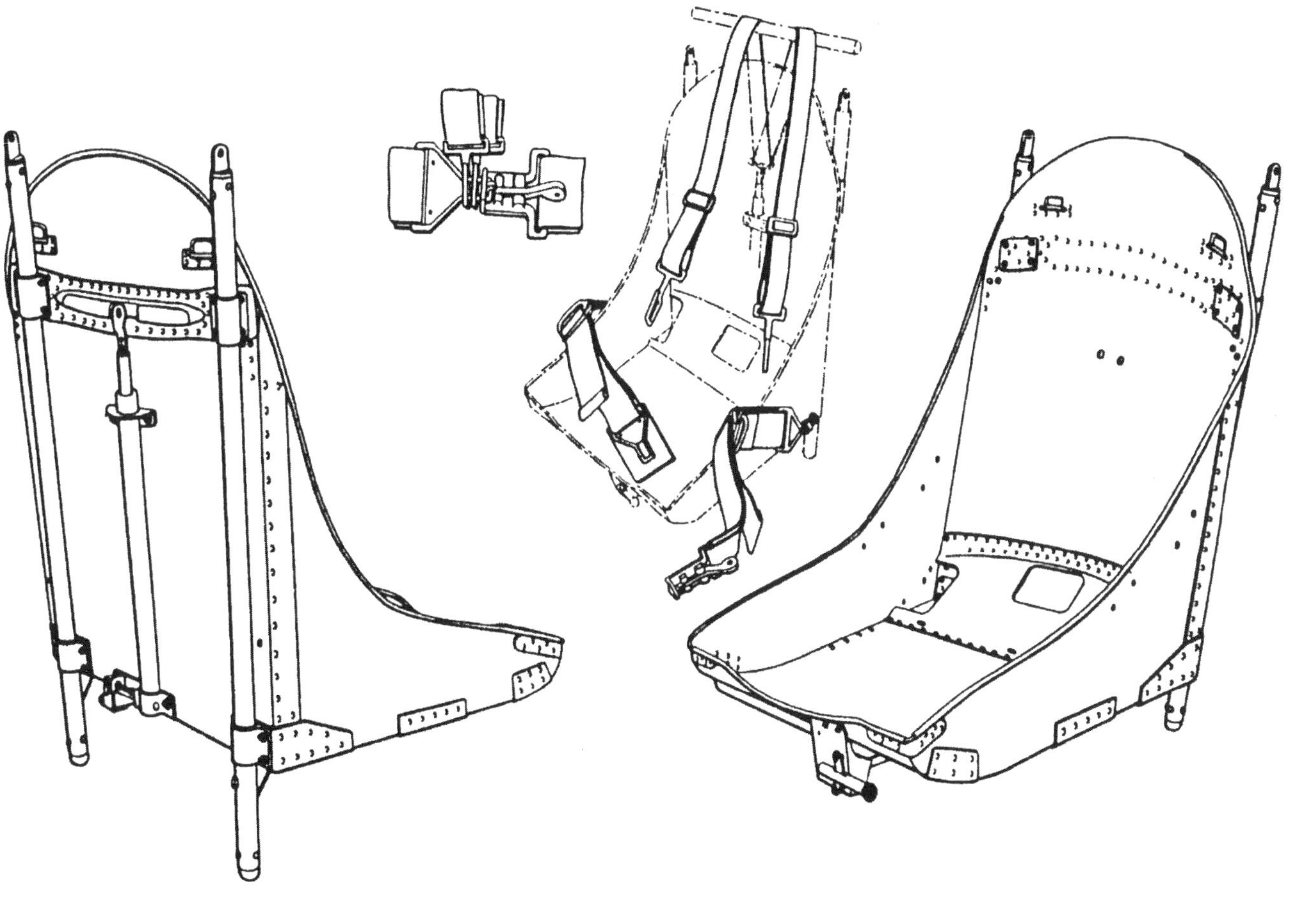

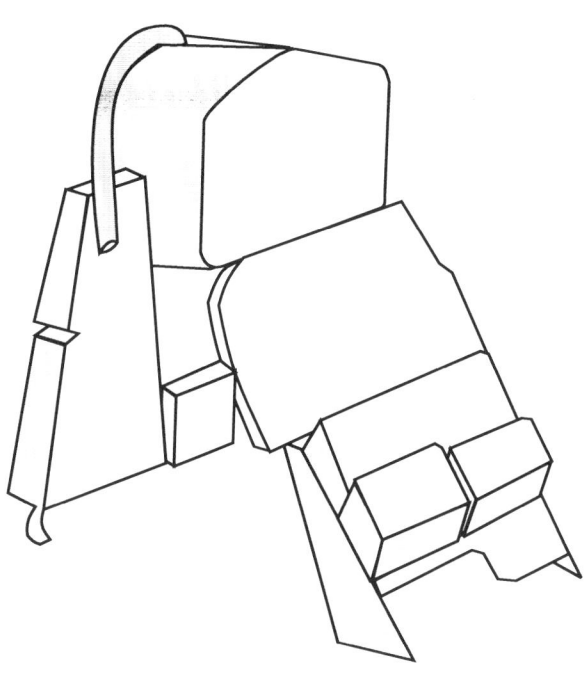
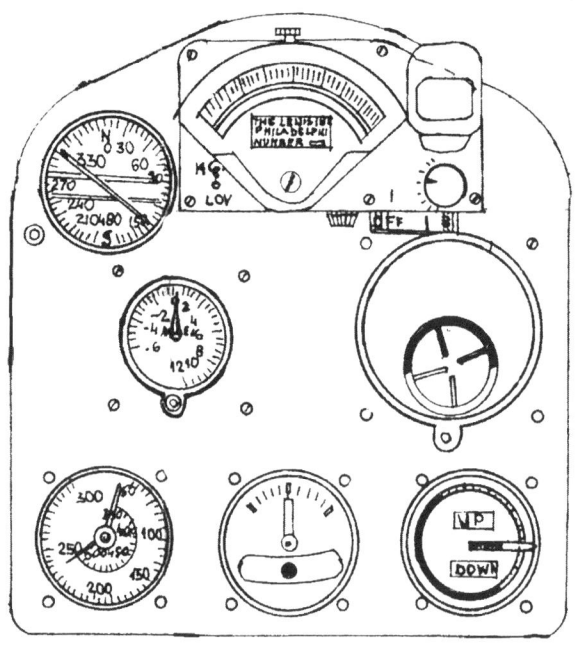

Details of the instrument panels of P-39Q.

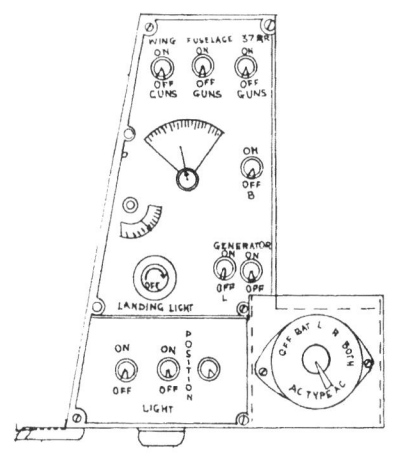
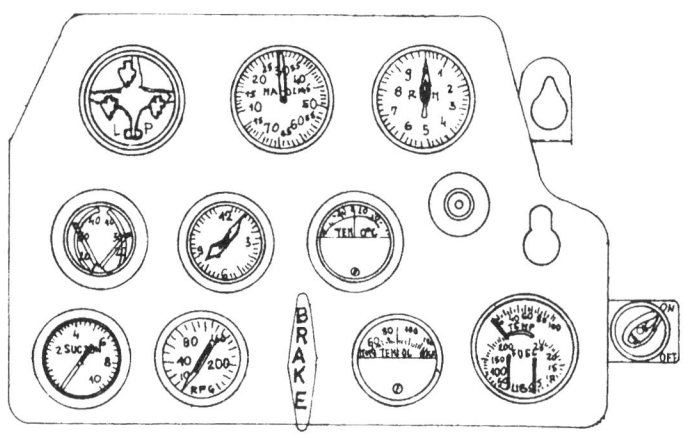

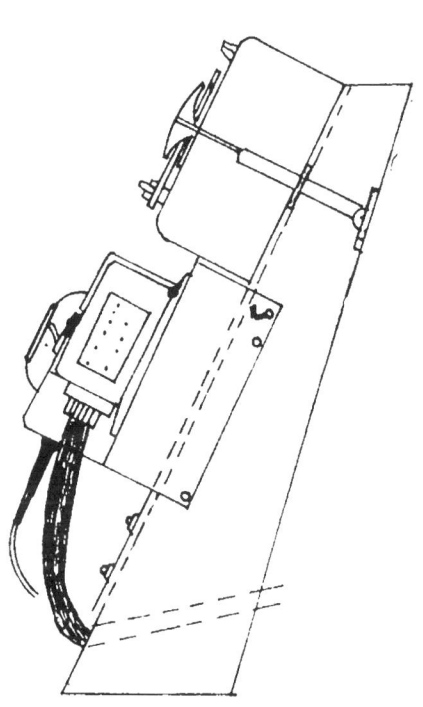
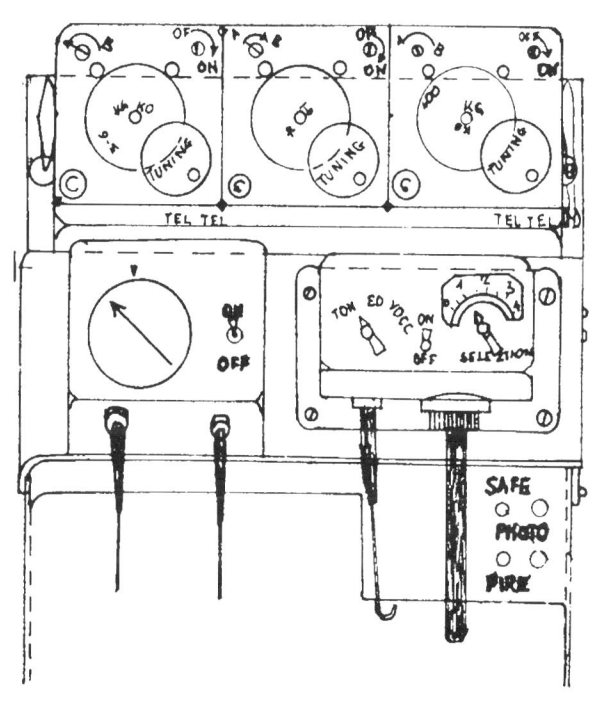

Right: P-39N instrument panel. Just above control column the .50-caliber machine gun is visible. The red gun charging handle is also visible.

Bottom of the page:
The handle in the right corner is the landing gear emergency control crank. On the left is oil shutter control and the silver handle in the black housing on the floor is the coolant shutter control.

Opposite page:
Top, left: P-39N instrument panel with N-3 gunsight on the top. In front of the gunsight is the rubber crash pad to protect the pilot.

Top right: Port side door. Open crank (red) is visible and handle to raise and lowered the window (also red, but the lower one).

Bottom left:
Details of the left part of the instrument panel and centre console.

Bottom right:
Inside of the starboard door, very similar to port one. Data and map case is also visible with fixed instructions how to operate landing gear and flaps.

(All photos A. Lochte)

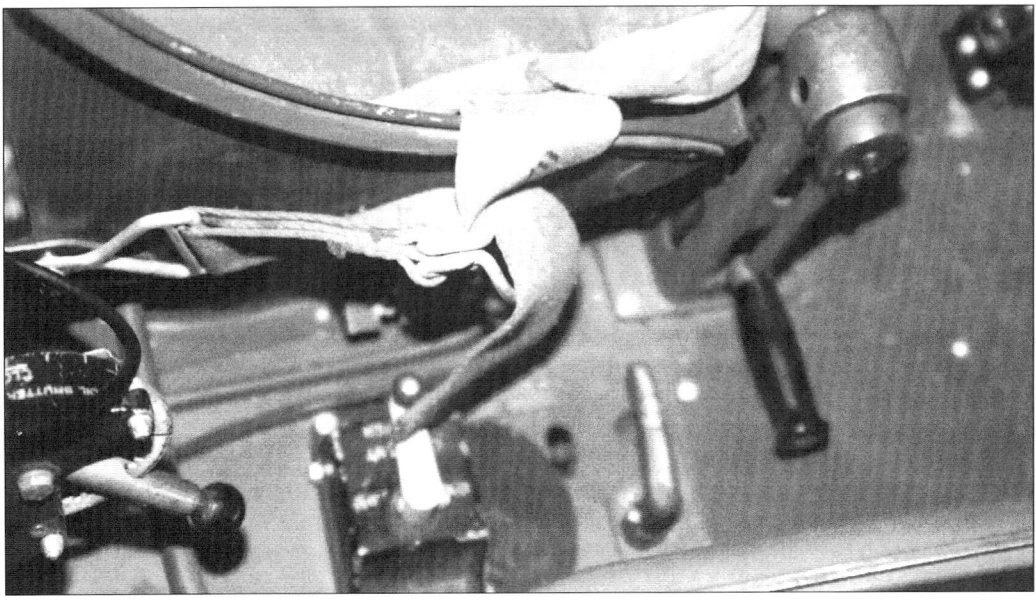

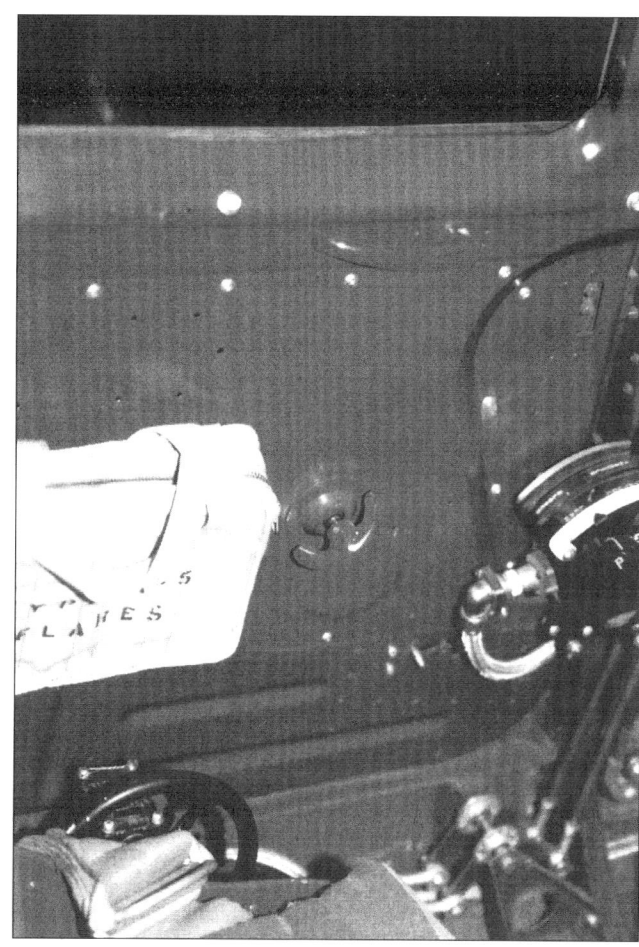

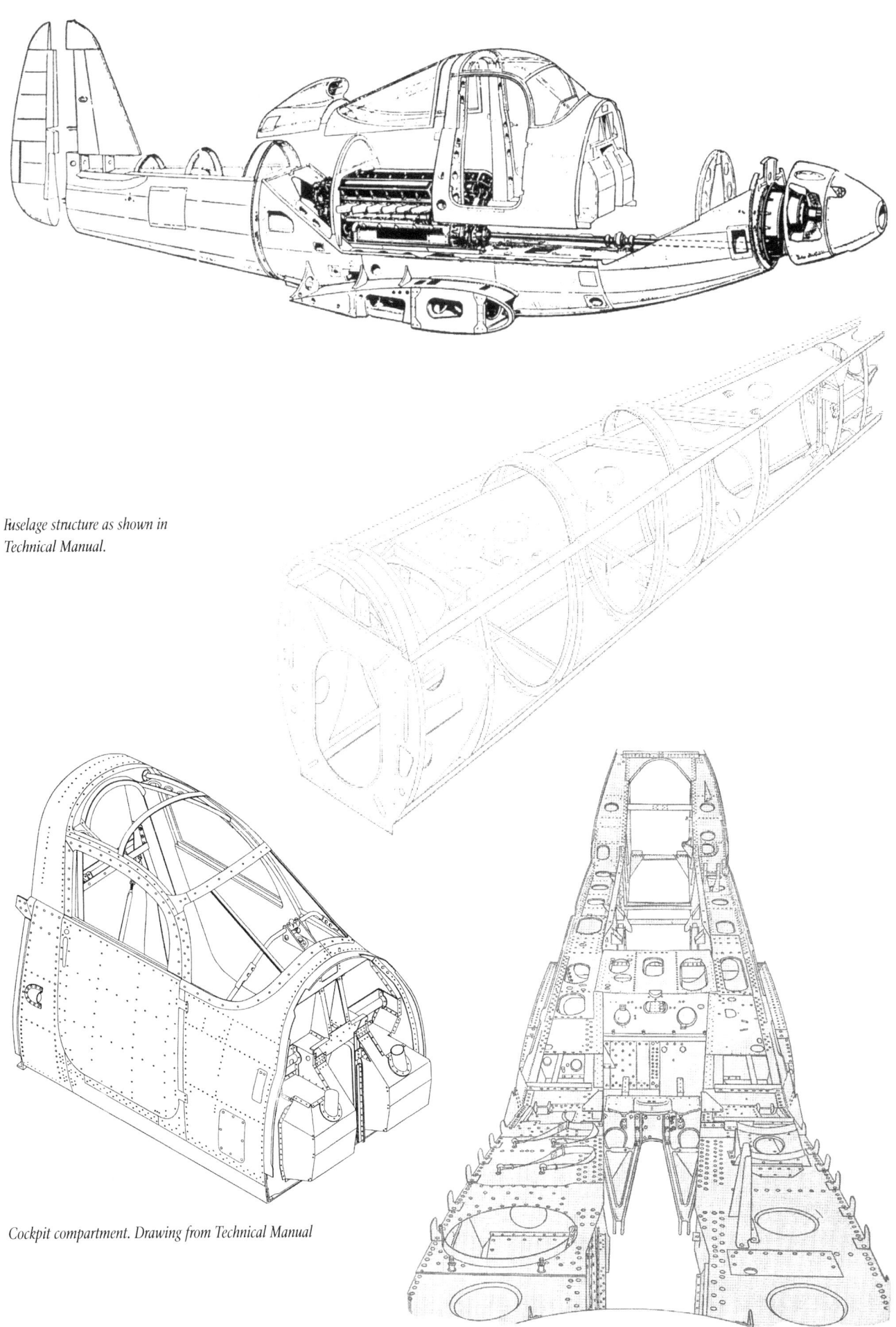

Fuselage structure as shown in
Technical Manual.

Cockpit compartment. Drawing from Technical Manual

Engine maintenance. (US National Archive)

Airacobra during overhaul. (US National Archive)

P-39Q-5, serial 42-20381 of 7th AF piloted by John M. Maxwell. (US National Archive)

P-39Q-1, serial 42-19549, "Tarawa Boom De-Ay" of the 318th FG, Oahu, Hawaii. (US National Archive)

P-39Q-20, '20', "Maxine". (Stratus coll.)

P-39Q-20, serial 44-3569 of the 71st TRG, 82nd TRS. Personal aircraft of 1st Lt. Carl T. Bailey, 1944. Note redesigned nose wheel hub. (via A. Lochte)

P-39Q-10, serial 42-20581 in Soviet markings. This aircraft is fitted with the long-range external fuel tank. (Stratus coll.)

Two P-39Qs taking off at one of the Pacific island. (US National Archive)

P-39Q at Bougainville, Solomon Islands. (US National Archive)

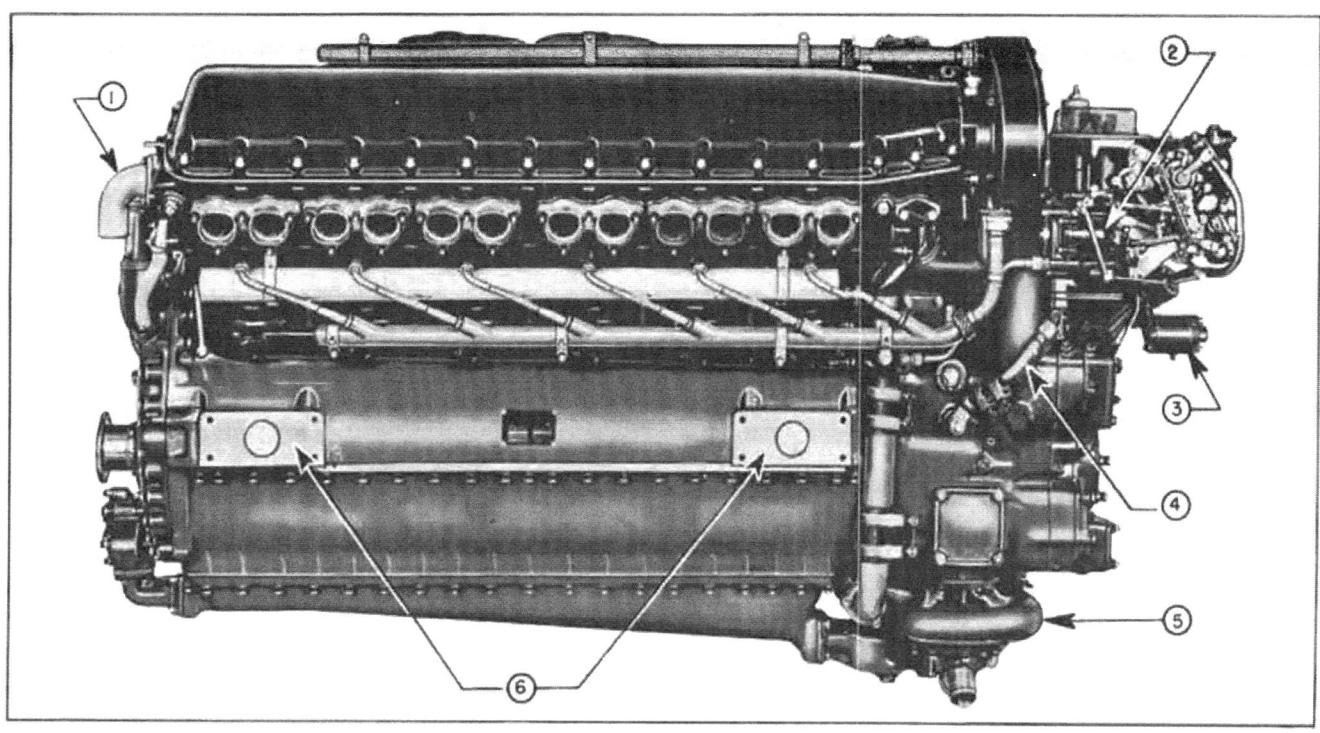

Figure 4—Left Side View—V-1710-63, -83, or -85 Model Engine

1—Coolant Outlet Elbow
2—Automatic Manifold Pressure Regulator
3—Carburetor Nozzle Accelerating Pump
4—Regulator Oil Drain Tube
5—Coolant Pump
6—Engine Mounting Pads

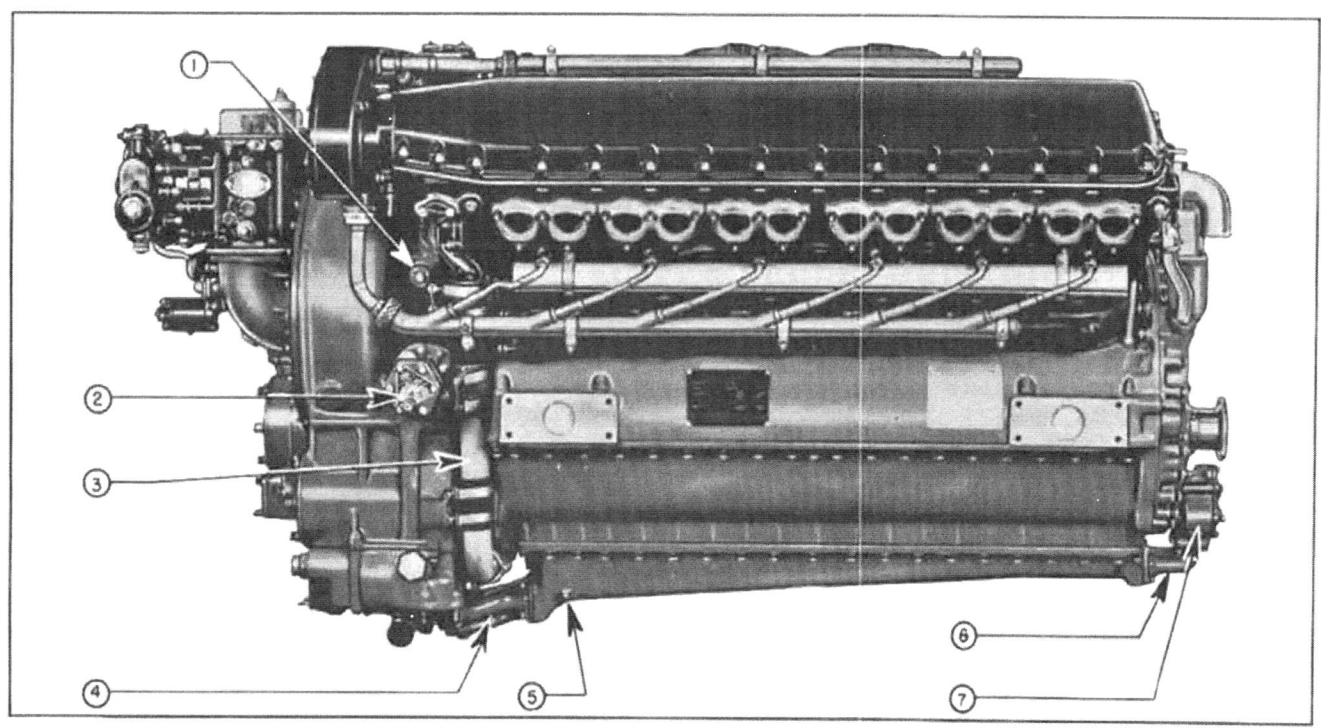

Figure 5—Right Side View—V-1710-63, -83, or -85 Model Engine

1—Optional Vacuum Pump Oil Return Connection
2—Oil Strainer
3—Coolant Pipe to R. H. Block
4—Rear Oil Drain Elbow
5—Hydraulic Acc. Oil Return Conn.
6—Front Oil Drain Elbow
7—Front Scavenger Oil Pump

15

Nose of the P-39Q. (M. Orlog)

Photo of the right, middle part of the fuselage. (M. Orlog)

*Details of the engine covers and air intake, from the right.
(M. Orlog)*

P-39Q, bottom of the nose, port side. (A. Lochte)

Left: *Details of the direction-finder loop mounted on Soviet Airacobras. (M. Orlog)*

Aerial mounting at the top of the fuselage. (M. Orlog)

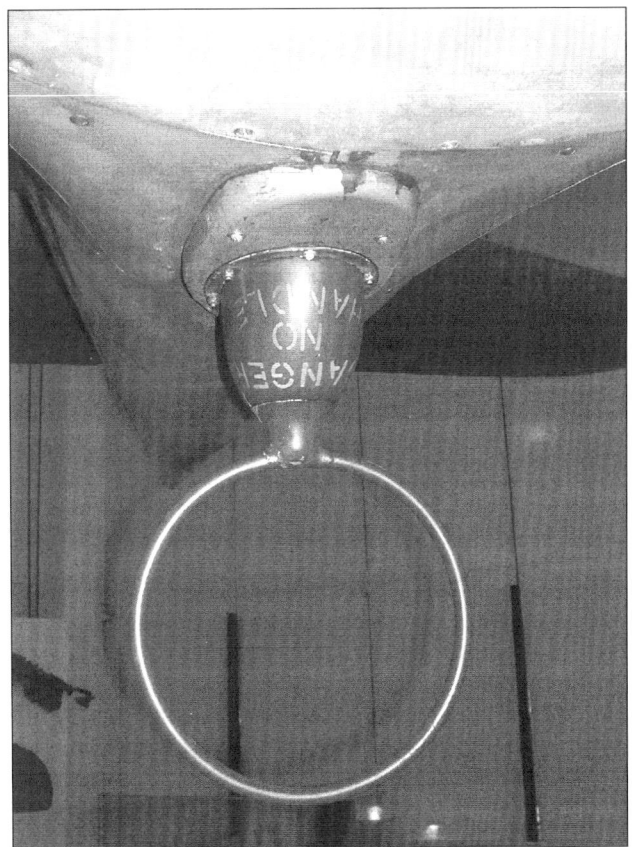

Two photos of the forward, starboard part of the fuselage. (All photos M. Orlog)

P-39Q, rear, port side of the fuselage. First Aid access panel is visible. (A. Lochte)

Prestone radiator with coolant shutter closed. Oil shutter on the left, also in closed position. P-39Q.

Series of three photos showing glycol cooler intake (inboard) and oil cooler intake (outboard). P-39Q. (All photos M. Orlog)

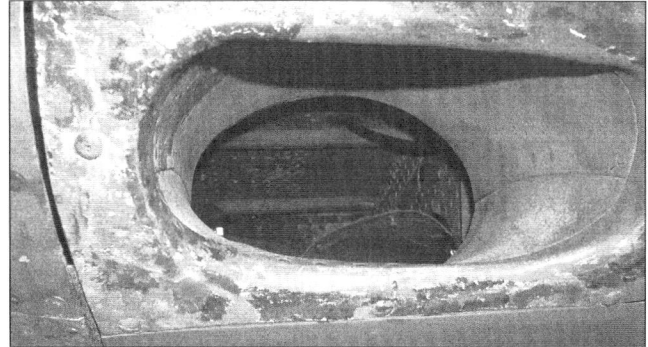

Nose of the P-39Q from the right. (M. Orlog)

P-39Q, lower part of the tail. (M. Orlog)

P-39Q rudder and fin. Note the trim tab and rudder hinge. In the right photo horizontal stabiliser's fairing is clearly visible.

Horizontal tailplane of the same aircraft. (Photos M. Orlog)

P-39Q, starboard tail fillet. (A. Lochte)

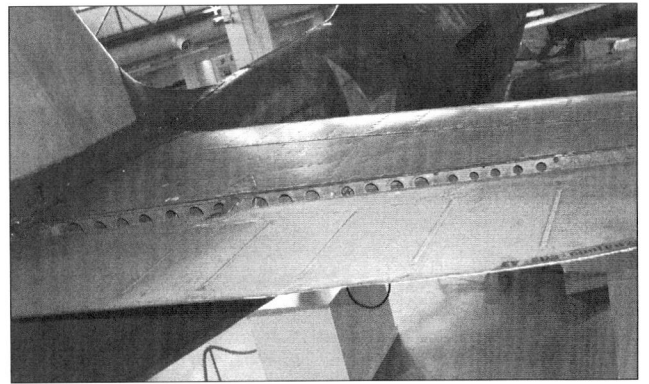

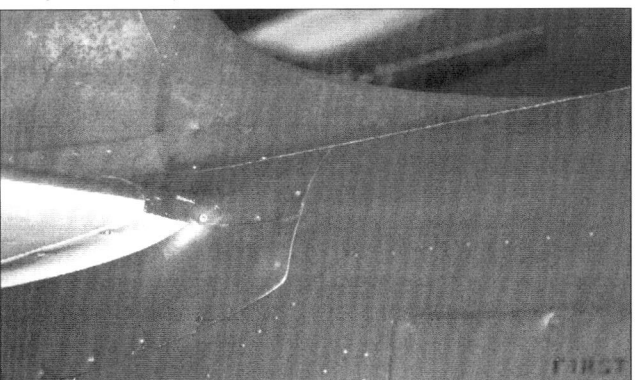

Inner end of the starboard landing flap. (A. Lochte photos)

Above, left: *front view of the main leg, looking aft.* **Above, right**: *Inside of the portside main undercarriage gear. Note details of the wheel hub disk of the P-39Q, different that of the P-39N shown in the photo on the page 93. (Photos R. Wallsgrove)*

P-39Q in Soviet markings. Aircraft preserved in Finnish Museum Keski-Suomen Ilmailumuseo in Tikkakoski. Aircraft still in original camouflage (not repainted in museum, after the war). Note that Soviet P-39Q were not fitted with underwing guns. (All photos M. Orlog)

Two photos of the armament compartment of the P-39N. Note that .50 cal machine gun ammunition box is missing. Aircraft during restoration. (A. Lochte)

Two photos of P-39 undersurfaces. Note the early WWII markings - "US ARMY".
This is a P-39Q altered to represent an earlier Airacobra variant. For example, mockups of the wing guns are visible.
(A. Lochte)

P-39Q of 19 GIAP, end of 1943. Personal aircraft of Capt. Pavel Kutashov (13+28 victories). Olive Drab over Neutral Grey.

Artur Juszczak

23